HAPPY
Birthday
imagination

Happy birthday, Puffin!

Did you know that in 1940 the very first Puffin story book (about a man with broomstick arms called Worzel Gummidge) was published? That's 70 years ago! Since then the little Puffin logo has become one of the most recognized book brands in the world and Puffin has established its place in the hearts of millions.

And in 2010 we are celebrating 70 spectacular years of Puffin and its books! Pocket Money Puffins is a brand-new collection from your favourite authors at a pocket-money price – in a perfect pocket size. We hope you enjoy these exciting stories and we hope you'll join us in celebrating the very best books for children. We may be 70 years old (sounds ancient, doesn't it?) but Puffin has never been so lively and fun.

There really IS a Puffin book for everyone

Meg Rosoff became a publishing sensation after her first novel *How I Live Now* won the Guardian Children's Fiction Prize. Her second novel, *Just in Case*, won the highly prestigious Carnegie Medal in 2007 and *What I Was*, her third novel, was shortlisted for the Carnegie Medal and was highly acclaimed. Her latest novel is *The Bride's Farewell*, published in 2009.

Books by Meg Rosoff

HOW I LIVE NOW

JUST IN CASE

WHAT I WAS

THE BRIDE'S FAREWELL

VAMOOSE!

meg rosoff

VAMOOSE!

PUFFIN

PUFFIN BOOKS

Published by the Penguin Group

Penguin Books Ltd, 80 Strand, London WC2R ORL, England

Penguin Group (USA) Inc., 375 Hudson Street, New York, New York 10014, USA

Penguin Group (Canada), 90 Eglinton Avenue East, Suite 700, Toronto, Ontario, Canada M4P 2Y3
(a division of Pearson Penguin Canada Inc.)

Penguin Ireland, 25 St Stephen's Green, Dublin 2, Ireland (a division of Penguin Books Ltd)

Penguin Group (Australia), 250 Camberwell Road, Camberwell, Victoria 3124, Australia
(a division of Pearson Australia Group Pty Ltd)

Penguin Books India Pvt Ltd, 11 Community Centre, Panchsheel Park, New Delhi – 110 017, India

Penguin Group (NZ), 67 Apollo Drive, Rosedale, North Shore 0632, New Zealand
(a division of Pearson New Zealand Ltd)

Penguin Books (South Africa) (Pty) Ltd, 24 Sturdee Avenue, Rosebank,
Johannesburg 2196, South Africa

Penguin Books Ltd, Registered Offices: 80 Strand, London WC2R ORL, England

puffinbooks.com

First published 2010

1

Text copyright © Meg Rosoff, 2010
Colour Puffin artwork on cover copyright © Jill McDonald, 1974
All rights reserved

The moral right of the author and illustrator has been asserted

Set in Adobe Caslon 11.75/19pt
Typeset by Ellipsis Books Limited, Glasgow
Made and printed in England by Clays Ltd, St Ives plc

British Library Cataloguing in Publication Data
A CIP catalogue record for this book is available from the British Library

ISBN: 978-0-141-32914-7

www.greenpenguin.co.uk

For Ivor and Matilda

Contents

Vamoose!

The midwife was giving me the evil eye.

'Mothers your age often have trouble bonding,' she said, and then added grudgingly, 'but it will come.'

My age? Jeez. It's not like I was twelve or something.

We'd spent the last ten minutes glaring at each other, but I couldn't help admiring the way she cradled my baby, holding him close up against her great big bazooms and looking into his big velvety eyes. Also, her smile (at him) appeared to be genuine. Which was a plus.

'Who's a dear little sweet thing?' she cooed. 'Who's a beautiful big moosie boy?' My baby held her gaze adoringly, eyes unblinking. 'Look at those eyelashes!' She turned to me. 'Well, he may not be what you expected, but he *is* a beauty.'

'I wish you'd tell that to my mum.' Squinting, I searched for the beauty in the curve of his nose, his little baby nostrils. 'She refuses to look at him. I guess she has a point. He is kind of hairy.'

'Don't you mind about that, now. Just look at his lovely wee hooves.'

The midwife held out one tiny foot, shiny and ebony black. It *was* cute. I closed my eyes, still pretty numb and queasy from the Caesarean. And a little dizzy from getting used to things. I mean, how exactly had this happened? The twenty-week scan was perfectly normal.

'It's a late development in some pregnancies,' the consultant said in his I'm-SO-much-more-important-than-you voice, slithering out of any and all blame

4

at the same time. 'We often fail to pick it up on the blood test.' He paused. 'They're not common, but we've had a small cluster of non-homo-sapien births this year. Mainly moose. No one knows why.'

I squeezed my eyes into slits and suddenly realized that he wasn't a doctor at all, he was a zombie! Heh heh. Of course he hadn't looked so superior when Mum threatened to sue the hospital over my non-homo-sapien birth. He'd looked even queasier than I felt.

'Something to help you sleep?' A slightly elevated eyebrow suggested that he'd accept if it were *his* child. 'We'll send the social worker round first thing in the morning. In the meantime, try to get some rest. It won't look so bleak in daylight.'

Was he referring to the situation or my baby? I didn't think either was going to look a whole lot better in the clear light of day.

* * * *

'Well, I guess we can't call him Imogen.' Nick stared at the furry creature in the cot. I could understand his disappointment. We'd both been convinced we were having a girl. And a human being.

'What do you suggest? We have to call him something. Lucien doesn't seem right either.'

'Bullwinkle?'

'Hilarious, Nick.'

But when I turned back to him, he looked glum. 'What on earth am I going to tell my parents?'

'Yeah, that's our biggest worry. Gimme the phone, I'll break the news. "Hello, Anthony? Camille? Your son's girlfriend's given birth to a bouncing baby moose. Ten point two kilos – by Caesarean section, in case you were wondering, and yeah, *that's* why I got so fat. Big floppy ears and lots of hair. Mother and son doing well. Boyfriend not so good."'

I don't know what I expected, but he seemed really stricken. I sighed. 'Look, Nick, they'll cope. It's us I'm worried about.' I reached over and took his hand – it seemed only kind. In the plastic cot beside me, Baby Moose Pearson slept wrapped up in a pale blue hospital blanket. None of the cute Babygros I'd bought fitted. He muttered and squeaked in his sleep, his floppy nose wrinkling and unwrinkling.

Tears filled Nick's eyes. 'My son.'

'What about Moe?'

'Moe Moose?' Nick stared at me. 'Have you ever *been* to a playground?'

'Moe Pearson, actually.' But I took his point.

My phone rang and Nick answered. 'It's your mum.'

I shook my head.

'She's asleep,' he lied, then listened for a minute. 'OK, I'll tell her.' He rang off and handed back my phone. 'She says she loves you no matter what, but that you're really pushing it this time.'

'Did you mention that it wasn't my idea to give birth to a moose?'

Nick shrugged. 'She probably knows that.'

Suddenly Nick seemed to remember that this hadn't been a great day for me either. 'My poor Jess.' He sat on the edge of the bed and hugged me clumsily, avoiding the drip. 'What a time you've had.'

Too right. My eyes drooped as a new nurse swept through the door, a large woman in a striped pinafore. 'Baby Boy Pearson? I've got him on my list for a special feed.' Her accent was Irish. She peered into the plastic cot and her face split into a huge grin. 'Well, well, well. Will you look at that little thing.' She lifted him out of the cot with a comedy groan, and laid him expertly in the curve of her arm. 'Excuse me, not so little. Who's a sweet boy then? Who's the sweetest handsomest boy?'

I tried to see him through her eyes. He *was* cute. He looked like one of those oversized cuddly toys you might buy at Hamley's. To stick at the end of a proper baby's cot. I closed my eyes.

'Look, Jess, I think I'd better get going.'

I nodded. So tired.

'Night, night.' Nick seemed reluctant to let go of my hand. 'I'll be back first thing.'

'Uh-huh.'

Seventeen. Pregnant. And now this. Oblivion was definitely my best option.

* * * *

'What about Rudolph?'

'I see you've got your sense of humour back.' I was holding my baby, sitting up in a chair, leaning him against my chest, as the Breast-Feeding Facilitator had demonstrated. But it was no good. He showed no desire to latch on, despite having more than enough lip for the job. Nick put him back in his cot.

'So . . . nothing's changed?' His question was totally pathetic. What had he been expecting? A letter from the hospital? 'Sorry, folks, we made a mistake. Your moose actually belongs to a large female ruminant who checked in around the same time you did.'

'Nope.' I indicated the bundle. 'Nurse said he drank like a sailor in the night.'

'That's my boy.' For a second Nick actually looked proud.

'But he isn't farting and begging for aspirin this morning, so maybe he takes after someone else.'

'Rudolph. Rudy.' Nick tried the name out, giggling. 'Reminds me of a really fit guy in tights doing jetés with a great big bulging –'

'Stop that image *right now*, before it sticks. Maybe we should go back to one of the names we thought of before.'

'Oh no, please. Not Lucien.'

'So?'

'How 'bout Mickey? *Mickey Moose?*' Nick doubled over, hysterical.

I'd have sacrificed every one of my eighteen stitches to punch him just then, but he was saved by the arrival of Mum, followed closely by Marion Streatham, Medical Social Worker.

'You must be Jessica Pearson?'

I could see her running down a checklist in her head: *Teen mother. Multiple piercings. Weird tattoo. Post-natal depression. Failure to bond. Inadequate parenting skills.* I didn't have to guess at Mum's checklist: *Kill Nick. Kill me. Send moose baby to zoo.*

'Hi, Mum.'

'Hello, sweetheart. Did you get some sleep?' I could tell Mum had made up her mind to be nice in front of the social worker.

'Pills.' I held up the little packet they'd left me.

'*Now* you're taking pills?'

Shoulda seen that one coming.

My eyes met Miss Streatham's and she looked away. I bet she never had to deal with three generations of a moose family before.

'Well . . .' she began, hesitantly. 'So this is baby . . .?'

'Rudolph,' I said, and out of the corner of my eye, saw Nick wince.

'Would you like to hold him, Mum?'

'*Don't call me mum.*' There was only one mum in this room and that was the one glaring at me through the world's fakest smile. And anyway, the short answer was no, I didn't want to hold him. What I wanted to hold was a baby like everyone else had. Or better yet, a box of Krispy Kremes.

She put down her notebook and lifted him out of the cot, grunting a bit.

'There you go, Mum.' Broad, patronizing smile. 'Isn't he precious?'

I took him, glaring at her. 'Do you have kids, Ms . . .' I peered at her name-tag. 'Streatham?'

She smiled her best druid hippy smile. 'I've always surrounded myself with little ones.'

Little ones? I nearly gagged. 'Did any of those little ones have hooves?' I lifted one of Rudolph's skinny moose legs and waved it in her direction.

'No.' She glanced heavenward. 'But I'd have loved them just the same if they had.'

'MUM!'

Mum took her by the arm and led her towards the door. 'Jess can be a bit moody,' she whispered loud enough for me to hear.

'Get her out of here!' I wanted to kill them both.

Mum gave me a look that said, 'Well, this is just the sort of conversation you get into when you don't listen to me about having sex and are too much of an irresponsible know-all to remember to use contraception properly, so, frankly, it serves you right – after all, it wasn't *me* who suggested you get knocked up by that useless posh boy.'

My mum's got a very expressive face.

Then she sighed and said she was going for a cappuccino and did anyone want one? But by the time I said yeah, I could murder a double mocha latte, she'd scarpered.

'Miss Pearson –' The social worker, ever-game, was creeping back into the ring.

'Jess.'

'Miss Pearson, is this –' I could tell she was about to say 'boy' – 'is this *person* the baby's father?'

Nick clearly hated her as much as I did, which made me remember why I loved him, if only for a moment.

'*She* says I am,' he said, pointing an accusatory finger at me. 'But I think she's lying. There are all sorts in my line – Orthodox Jews, Rastafarians, pygmies. But not a single moose.' He crossed his arms. Over to you.

I sniggered. 'Don't look at me. High church top to bottom. Nothing suspect anywhere.'

Poor Miss Streatham finally appeared to be getting flustered. I flashed Nick a smile. Score. She made a note in her notebook and pushed a strand of mousy hair behind one ear. 'I'd like us to try a little bonding exercise. Mum, hold Baby on your lap; Dad, you stand behind her and to the left, looking over the shoulder at your baby. I want you both to mirror each of his little movements and expressions.' She took a step backwards and tried out her beatific smile. It came out crooked.

Nick and I stared intently at our baby, who stiffened suddenly, a far-away look in his eye. And then there was a kind of trumpeting *phlapppppppp* accompanied by the pungent foresty smell of . . . of moose poo.

I glared at her. 'I'm not mirroring that.'

'Motherhood is full of Unique Challenges,' she said piously. 'We'll just change Baby's nappy and start again. Try to maintain eye contact throughout.'

I tried, but failed. Scraping a bucket of poo off a furry animal is enough of a Unique Challenge with both eyes trained on the job.

When Miss Streatham finally left, she looked utterly done in. Nick and I, on the other hand, had cheered up considerably.

'We might have to make it work,' he said. 'Just to ward off social workers.'

I giggled and made a cross with my fingers. 'Like vampires.'

Nick picked Moosie up out of the cot, lifted him to eye-level and slipped seamlessly from his own voice into his dad's. 'Of course we'll have to put him down for Eton.'

I grimaced and thought of the cute little sheepskin baby booties Jasmine had bought on the school trip to Wales – only two, and completely the wrong shape.

The Unique Challenges were coming fast and furious.

* * * *

Moosie was six weeks old when we were invited to meet other members of our non-homo-sapien baby 'cluster'. The first meeting was in Richmond, in a big look-how-posh-we-are house owned by a lawyer and her husband. There were seven parents at the meeting, three couples and me. They were all about Mum's age, which freaked me out from the start. I was already seething with resentment that Nick wasn't there. Liverpool were playing, but he'd *definitely* come next time.

Yeah.

Our baby had been up and walking more or less from birth, sticking his funny nose into everything. I can't say I was getting used to motherhood, but I was doing what was required to keep both of us alive and out of jail.

I fed him a diet of fortified cow's milk topped up with fresh grass and twigs, and he was already the size of a small pony. At local baby groups he was viewed with almost as much suspicion as I was, but the truth was that the other babies adored him. They shrieked with joy when he arrived, fought to chew on his tail or grab his floppy ears, and giggled uncontrollably at the noises that emerged from his moosey bottom. He was such a sweet furry thing, gentle and friendly and shy, that after a while the snide comments from other carers tapered off. Towards him, at least. They were still desperate to say, 'of course *that's* what comes of having kids too young' to me.

Mum wouldn't admit it but I could tell she liked having him around, and after I screamed four hundred million times that I wasn't putting him up for adoption, she backed off. She comes on like a dragon, my mum, but underneath she's a dragon. And about ten thousand leagues under that, she's mush.

It was Mum's idea that I bond with other animal-baby parents. Apparently there'd been articles in the paper, and there was even an organization: Parents Of Non-homo-sapien Young (PONY). But you don't notice that kind of stuff if you mostly read music mags. Mum left the *Guardian* open on the kitchen table to a double-page spread with a picture of a cheery couple and their bouncing moose baby all decked out in designer baby clothes, so he just seemed like part of a cool new trend. When I refused even to read it, she emailed the address at the bottom of the article and got an answer back right away inviting me 'and my husband or partner' to PONY's monthly meeting.

Mum accompanied us right to the door so I couldn't escape and I recognized the woman who opened it from the newspaper article. She had a big boy moose and a pretty little blonde toddler tugging at her skirt. 'Come in, come in,' she said, looking from Mum to Moosie to me, desperately trying to untangle the relationships. But Mum skedaddled, leaving her more puzzled than ever and me standing on the doorstep like that painting of *The Scream*.

The woman didn't seem to notice. 'Hello! I'm Alice. Marc is somewhere, and this is Sebastian,' she indicated the moose baby and his non-moose sister, 'and Molly.'

'This is Lucien Imogen Rudolph,' I told her, 'but we call him Moosie.'

Alice ushered us into a big living-room with white sofas and a huge square Italian coffee table. She started to offer me wine, but on second thought steered me towards the apple juice instead. Moosie hovered politely at the edge of a game of Buckaroo, waiting for a chance to play. One or two parents commented on what good manners he had.

'Of course he's still young,' Alice said with a sigh. 'Sebastian was an absolute love at his age.'

What did she mean? Despite his stupid designer clothes, Sebastian still seemed like a sweet little moose.

The large woman sitting next to me introduced herself as Mona. When Alice disappeared into the kitchen, she said in a low voice, 'He disembowelled their Labrador.'

Whoa.

'Of course,' continued Mona, smiling fakely, 'some

non-homo-sapien babies are more difficult than others. Moose babies can be particularly wearing.'

To prove her point, she called her baby and he waddled over. 'This is Viktor, our youngest. We haven't had a minute's trouble with him.' She lowered her voice. 'I think it's because we treat him just exactly the same as our other children. We don't want Viktor ever to feel different, do we, Craig dear?'

'I'm not even sure he realizes he *is* different,' chuckled Craig Dear.

Viktor was an emu. Mona and Craig were freaks.

The fourth family, Ari and Sarah Birnbaum, had three little boys with earlocks and yarmulkes, and Rivka, a little girl moose. She was dressed in a ruffled yellow pinafore, with little yellow striped padders on her feet. I wondered if moose was even kosher.

Moosie and Rivka looked as if they were going to play nicely together until Moosie pulled Rivka's dress off with his teeth. Sarah snatched her daughter out of harm's way.

'See what I mean,' hissed Mona. 'You'll have to keep an eye on him when he's in rut.'

My baby? *In rut?* I was going to be sick.

'Now that we're all assembled,' Marc said, tapping for silence on his wine glass, 'perhaps we should open the meeting.' He turned to Alice, who stood.

'First of all, a warm welcome to our newcomers. As you're no doubt in the process of discovering, having a non-homo-sapien child can be a unique challenge for any family, and a unique joy, too.'

Oh God, not another Unique Challenge.

Alice paused, her face stern, as if daring us not to experience all the various forms of uniqueness. 'It is only by embracing life's wondrous gifts that each of us can begin to fulfil our individual destinies.'

Hoo boy, I thought, missing Nick. I peered around the room, desperate for a soulmate – someone, anyone, doing eye-rolling and lip-curling. But it was obvious I was the only one who heard words like 'wondrous gifts' and 'individual destinies' and wanted to barf.

'The point is,' she continued, 'that together we must fight for our children to be treated as equals.'

'No special schools?' Craig asked worriedly.

'Absolutely not. When the time comes, Sebastian will be mainstreamed, perhaps with a helper to surmount some of the challenges –'

Sarah raised her hand. 'What sort of challenges are you anticipating?'

'I'm glad you asked.' Alice pulled out a neatly typed sheet of A4 paper and began to recite. '*Aggression, arithmetic, art classes, batting at games, binary numbers, bird watching, bonding with other children, carol singing, calculus, chemistry . . . handwriting, homework . . .*'

I drifted into a coma, but no one seemed to notice.

'*. . . long division, logarithms . . .*' On and on she droned, ending, appropriately enough, with 'zoo visits', after which there was a stunned silence. Moosie, a child after my own heart when it came to attention-seeking behaviour, grabbed the moment by squatting slightly and emitting a great squirting stream of green poo on to Alice and Marc's fluffy white Anatolian lamb rug.

Oops. Had she mentioned potty training while I dozed? I swept the cheerful moose out of the room, muttering something about him having a funny tummy, while Rivka's mother started to retch.

'Let's blow this joint, Moosie,' I whispered into his furry ear. 'Dunno about you, but I'm not ready to sign up for the WI.'

Mum was waiting for us around the corner at Starbucks. The ride home was a little on the silent side.

* * * *

I'd been hoping to go back to school when my baby was six months old, but things weren't going to plan. For one thing, try finding a crèche or a childminder who'll take a moose. And Mum wasn't quitting her job to take care of my baby – she'd made that totally clear when I first told her I was pregnant. Not that I blamed her. Being a human resources manager for a mid-range financial services marketing consultancy was probably *way* more fun than playing with a moose baby all day.

In any case, Moosie was getting to be a real handful. By four months he tipped the scales at eighty-five kilos and hurtled around the house in a gallop that shook the floors, knocked glasses off shelves and got all the lamps swinging. He loved it when I shouted, 'Hi ho, Moosie, and away!' but after a while it threatened to bring down the place, so I stopped.

His toilet habits were another problem. Nick came over after college every day and taught him to go in the garden, but for some reason I found this depressing. Especially when people came to visit, and in the middle of me showing them how cute he was playing with his toy rabbit, he'd leap to his feet with a bellow, and head out the back door for a poo. It kind of trashed the subtle message I'd got going, that he was a perfectly normal baby who just happened to be a moose.

Having a moose baby can tell you all sorts of things you might not have suspected about the grandparents. For all her hard line that if I was old enough to get pregnant, I was old enough to bring up my own baby, Mum began to show signs of surrender, knitting little Bambi-sized blankets and strawberry-shaped beanies. Moosie adored her, and did a special lolloping dance of happiness every time she came home from work that made the plaster fall off the ceiling. This was obviously my fault, cos she never seemed to blame Moosie for anything.

She started coming home early from the office to babysit and watch wildlife films with him, all cuddled up in bed and eating popcorn, which was what she and I always used to do together when I was little. 'Who's Grandma's best little moose?' Mum would ask, and Moosie would shoot me little smug looks that I swear said, 'well, it sure as heck ain't *you*'. I mean, is it normal to be snubbed by your own baby?

She read him *The Little Prince*, and *Mother Moose*, sorry, *Goose*, and tucked him into bed at night with 'Rock-a-Bye Baby', and his great big moosey eyelids would begin to droop with the first drowsy stages of sleep. Sometimes I'd hang around in the doorway thinking how infuriatingly cute they were together, but basically I was pleased they liked each other. It made my life easier, for one thing.

One Saturday afternoon, as Moosie lay snoring on the garden compost heap, I sat down next to Mum in the kitchen. 'I really do appreciate everything you do for Moosie,' I said. Which was true. And also I was hoping for a ticket to Glastonbury, which would mean I'd need Mum to babysit.

She took her specs off. 'What would you expect?

He's my only grandson. And haven't you noticed? He has my legs.'

'Be honest, Mum. Weren't you just a little disappointed when he was born?'

She fixed me, then, with her strong, wise gaze. 'Perhaps, just for a moment I was. But I knew I would grow to love him, just as I grew to love you and your sister.'

Funny turn of phrase, I thought.

My sister's twenty-four and lives in Australia and was really nice when she heard I was pregnant, not at all cross and superior. She has a little girl of her own and was excited when she heard Moosie was a boy. There was a long silence after we emailed the baby pictures, though. I think maybe she thought 'moose' was a term of endearment.

Nick's family weren't easy to win over either. His mum burst into tears more or less whenever Moosie's name was mentioned, but I tried not to take it personally. She'd had her heart set on a Cheltenham

Ladies College head girl for Nick, not a seventeen-year-old fertility goddess DJ he'd met at a rave. They clearly felt that I'd only got pregnant to ruin Nick's prospects of ever getting season tickets to Glyndebourne, so they didn't exactly welcome Moosie with open arms, but Nick insisted on bringing him to his house to stay some weekends so they could all learn to love each other.

Once or twice he caught his mum trying to teach Moosie how to use a fish-knife, which he thought was a great sign, but really the problems went deeper. Nick claimed they didn't care that they'd never be able to take Moosie to a garden party at Buckingham Palace, but when little silver teething rings and antique christening robes started arriving from the relatives, I suspected they weren't circulating pictures.

As for me – well, I loved Moosie. Of course I did. But I was also fairly stymied by a baby who stood five foot at the shoulder, and had fleas, and needed a specially reinforced concrete floor built for his playroom. Let's face it. I'd never really thought about having a toddler who chewed his cud.

'Where's my boy?' shouted Nick when he came in the door after school. And Moosie would slide head-first down the hall, occasionally breaking a bone in the arch of Nick's foot while dancing a sort of ecstatic moose pogo. Nick got used to being in plaster – the wild welcomes each evening resulted in one broken arm, a cracked cheekbone and three metatarsal fractures. They knew us at casualty now, and I got the feeling they blamed me for Nick's injuries, like just because of one small tattoo and a few eyebrow piercings, I might be one of those psychotic pit bull girlfriends, all nice one minute and woo-woo tear-your-throat-out the next. We never told them it was Moosie who was doing the damage in case social services got involved and took Nick away.

I admit I wondered whether Nick would ever look at me in that lovesick way he did way back when we first met, but most of the time I was either too busy or too tired to think about it much.

Sometimes late at night, Nick and I would stand together gazing down at our son, who lay snoring away in his sagging bed – *my* sagging bed actually – and then Nick would go home and I'd go and drag a duvet on to the sofa and stay up kind of wondering how I'd ended up on this particular winding road of life. I'm not saying it was a bad road exactly, it just wasn't the one I'd been expecting.

* * * *

Hanging around with your baby at home is completely different from suddenly having to send him to school. It's the difference between just being some kid with a baby and suddenly being a Parent, capital P. On the morning Nick and I took Moosie to my old primary school for the first time, it felt like a whole new chapter was beginning.

Most parents have three or four years to get used to the idea of their kid going to school, but at the rate Moosie was growing, we had to enrol him in nursery at just eight months. It totally weirded me out that my old nursery teacher, Miss Gillett, was still there, so I just tried to concentrate on Moosie, smart and proud in his new school uniform. Nick and I were both more nervous than he was.

'His socks are weird,' Nick hissed at me. 'Everyone's going to make fun of the way he looks.'

'They're tube socks, for God's sake. They're the only ones that fit.'

'And that polo shirt's all bunched up at his armpits.'

Did I look like Stella McCartney? 'Hey, Nick, I'm a DJ not a seamstress. I did my best.'

Nick bit his thumbnail. 'It's the little things that lead to bullying, you know. The wrong shirt, or football boots.'

Or antlers. Duh.

Miss Gillett, to give her credit, didn't make all the obvious jokes. Though she did look at me and say, 'I didn't expect to see you back in my classroom *quite* so soon.'

Me neither, to tell the truth. I shrugged. 'This is Moosie.'

I guess nursery teachers are trained not to throw up their hands in shock no matter what walks through the door, because she didn't blink. Our little moose was given his own cubbyhole with **LUCIEN** written above it in big block letters, and Miss Gillett took a Polaroid portrait of him to mount on the class board.

Nick was watching as a tiny Nigerian girl with perfect cornrows and a shy smile approached Moosie. 'Hello,' she said, clambering up on to the top of the reading cubicle partition to get closer to our son's eye-level. 'I'm Kiki.'

Moosie lowered his long velvety snout and snuffled in her ear. Kiki giggled, and Nick smiled at me. First day of school and already our son was friends with the coolest girl in the class. For one brief moment, we both felt optimistic. Even his toilet issues didn't freak out Miss Gillett. 'We'll just let him out two or three times each morning, so he can do his business in the wildlife garden,' she said with a no-nonsense smile. 'Not every child has the same needs.'

We were so happy.

But it didn't last. Within a week, the complaints started streaming in. There were crushed toes and bruises on the playground, and reports that our son had developed a habit of barricading himself in the pirate ship, bellowing at anyone who tried to play. Privately, I thought Kiki was egging on his bad behaviour, but of course it was impossible to prove. Things came to a head when Kiki's mum picked her up early from school one day, and according to the disciplinary report, Moosie leapt to his feet, charged at her with a great roar, and pinned her up against the wall 'in a terrifying and aggressive manner'.

'That's absurd,' Nick fumed. 'I'm sure it was just high spirits.'

At the exclusion meeting, they took one look at Moosie and made up their minds. The fact that he now weighed more than a hundred kilos convinced the committee that he didn't belong in a nursery class.

'But he's just a baby,' Nick pleaded.

Moosie pawed the floor and several governors looked frightened.

Miss Gillett said she was sorry to see him go. 'Perhaps you could bring him back when some of the other children have caught up with him, size-wise,' she said. But in our hearts, we knew it was not to be.

Nick raged about the unfairness of the system. 'Look at him! He's a perfectly happy kid. The slightest difference and they go all "I'm afraid we'll have to exclude him". They were prejudiced against him from the start.'

'He's a moose, Nicky.'

'I *know* he's a moose. But that doesn't mean he's some kind of freak.'

Nick's passionate defence of Moosie touched my heart. 'Actually, I think it does.'

He sighed. 'You know what I mean.'

I did. I took his hand and, with a deep breath, came out with it. 'Has it ever occurred to you that maybe . . .' I hesitated. After all this time, could I bring myself to say the unsayable? 'That maybe Moosie might be happier somewhere else?'

For an instant Nick perked up. 'Boarding school?'

'I was thinking more like . . . Canada?'

He pulled away, outraged. 'Never.'

With a single word, the subject was closed.

So, we got him on the special needs register and had him tested for dyslexia and dyspraxia, fought for speech therapists and reading tutors, and eventually had to accept that every person involved with his

36

education reached the same conclusion: Moosie's poor language skills and lack of an opposable thumb were holding him back.

Nick's parents had a friend whose cousin in Cambridge was a doctor specializing in hand surgery, and over Pimm's and strawberries at a Wimbledon party, they booked a consultation. As we sat in his plush Harley Street offices reading the testimonials, we discovered that he'd successfully performed thumb reconstruction on a number of industrial accident victims and Hollywood stars. It was a simple matter, he explained, of taking skin from the abdomen, implanting artificial ligaments, pulling nerves down into the new thumb-shaped appendage and hoping for the best. He warned us that it didn't work every time, and he'd never tried it on a hoof.

It sounded horrible. Nick was in favour of trying, I was definitely against. I couldn't bear to see Moosie turned into Frankenstein's monster, cut and scraped and shaped into something he wasn't. Next thing I knew we'd be talking about a nose job, having his ears tucked up to make him that little bit more like the other kids. The thought made me crazy.

'No.' I was adamant.

'What do you mean, no?'

'Just, no. I don't want him to go through all that pain when it's not going to work anyway. He's different. There's no point pretending he's not.'

'But he could learn to hold a pen, write poetry. He could play piano, or clarinet. How can you justify closing off the entire world of creative achievement to him?'

Every once in a while, Nick sounds like a total tit. It's not his fault though. If you met his parents you'd know what I mean.

'Nick,' I sighed, tired of the conversation, 'he's a moose. Moose don't play the clarinet.' I hated being the negative one all the time, but Nick's fantasy of his son in the wind section of the London Symphony

Orchestra was a little on the disturbing side as well.

* * * *

Moose children begin to show signs that adolescence is on the way between the ages of two and three. They will experience a huge growth spurt, will develop a strong musty odour, and may become moody and contrary. Most upsetting to some parents is the beginning of the first rutting season, heralded by a continuous loud croaking groan in boys.

So You Have a Moose Baby!

by Ann and Arnold Cooper, 4th edition

Our little Moosie was growing up.

As a two-year-old he'd spend hours staring out the window with a far-away, forlorn look in his huge liquid brown eyes, and I had to ask myself more and more often whether we were failing him. Home

39

schooling provided the stimulation his brain required, but what about a spiritual home? The sort of place where the buffalo roamed, and the deer and the antelope played. I was sure such a place existed. Canada still seemed the most likely prospect, but I'd looked into Norway, too. And Kamchatka.

Moosie now weighed 200kg and the facts of life were as follows: he was a boy moose. He needed a girl moose. For rutting. End of story. I couldn't be completely unsympathetic. I knew a lot of teenagers who felt the same way.

Nick and I still saw each other, and he was a good father to Moosie, but he was going off to university soon and I wasn't all that optimistic about us staying together. He said he still loved me, but everything he'd fallen in love with – the fact that I was the coolest person he'd ever met, by a factor of a hundred billion, for instance – had changed. I still kept up with new bands when I could, but late nights just wrecked me these days. OK, so I hadn't quite become one of those mothers who slopes off to the corner shop in her slippers for fags. But I could understand how you might be tempted.

Day after day, the terrible noise of an adolescent moose in rut filled our little area of south London. Moosie dug a rutting pit in the garden, peed in it five times a day, and splashed the muddy pee all over his body. He thought it made him smell hot, and I admired his confidence, but unfortunately, it didn't work. For one thing, there weren't many girl moose in our postcode. For another, there were the neighbours. We tried endlessly to explain, but after a while it seemed simpler just to stop answering the phone. I sat with Moosie for hours, trying to distract his attention with Sudoku, board games and papier mâché, but only old reruns on Wildlife TV interested him; he'd watch for hours hoping for some brief glimpse of a naked girl moose. My son was turning into a moody, morose teenager. Mum said I'd been exactly the same. Still was.

I couldn't cope. The GP sent me to someone with experience in depressed adolescents, and I found myself in a little office at our local mental health unit, talking to a middle-aged man. He offered me a seat and once I started talking I couldn't stop.

'Are you angry with your son,' he asked at last, 'for making your life so complicated?'

Angry? Yes, maybe I was. I was also angry at him for destroying most of the furniture in the house, filling every room with the stink of moose rut and shedding great handfuls of flea-ridden hair about the place. I was angry with him for stinking like a decomposed fox, and for making that great horrible noise all the time. I was angry at the fact that he thought about sex night and day, that he refused to devote himself to schoolwork, that he left great holes in the floor where he stamped his huge hooves . . .

But most of all, I was bloody pissed off that he was going through adolescence at the same time I was.

I began to sob uncontrollably. 'I love Moosie,' I gasped, 'I love him. But he's *such a nightmare to live with.*'

'I'm not doubting your love for him,' the therapist said quietly. 'I don't think love is the issue here. It won't change the way things are.'

I knew something about the way things were. They were bad.

'What am I going to do?' I wiped my eyes and blew my nose.

'Well,' he said, 'whatever you choose, we'll support you. But only you can decide what's best for both of you.'

I walked home, deep in thought.

Moosie began sneaking off to London Zoo at night, trumpeting his frustration to the camels and llamas. There was no female moose at the zoo, but the smell of the other ruminants drove him mad with desire.

The familiar 5 a.m. call from the night keeper woke

Nick, who staggered up to Camden with a lead rope and a bucket of Mars bars. When Moosie arrived home, I tried to stroke his head and rub his shoulders, but he shook me off and stormed off to his room. Nick sighed, and suggested I rub his shoulders instead.

'This isn't working,' he said at last.

'I'm not a professional masseuse.'

'Not the shoulders, the family.'

For a moment I held my breath.

'Maybe . . .'

There was a long silence.

'Maybe . . . we need to consider Canada again.'

I breathed out. 'Are you sure, Nick? Are you absolutely positively sure?'

He nodded and we clung together, our faces wet with tears. The time had come.

* * * *

I booked tickets for the three of us: Moosie in first class for the leg-room, Nick and me in economy. Nick's parents paid for the tickets. They were so enthusiastic about the plan that I nearly backed out.

Moosie enjoyed the champagne and the wide choice of nature programmes, but Nick and I didn't even bother with the films. I gazed out at the sun on the clouds and thought of the way my baby had snuggled into my arms and made me love him, the way he always put his little moosie snout on my shoulder and snuffled gently into my ear.

To any outsider, we were just an ordinary family setting off on an ordinary camping holiday to Desolation Bay . . . with two return tickets and one single. Nick squeezed my hand and I let my head droop onto his shoulder. Moosie had wandered back into steerage to see us and had fallen asleep across our seats, so we sat hunched together in the aisle. It had been this way all along: as Moosie grew, Nick and I shrank.

At passport control in Vancouver airport, the border guard looked carefully at our son's passport, at mine and Nick's, and back again. I waited for the inevitable challenge, but it didn't come. This was a country accustomed to moose. My mood picked up at once. We were making the right decision, for all of us.

As we trudged to the rental car agent's with our backpacks, Moosie's head swung this way and that, taking in all the new sights. He became so excited at the window displays filled with plush moose babies that we bought him one. He tucked it tenderly into his bum bag.

Eight hours later, I turned to look at Lucien Imogen Rudolph, crammed into the back seat of the compact rental car, the hard bony branches of his adolescent antlers scraping the roof, his nose laid gently up against his new cuddly toy. I kept my eyes peeled for movement beside the highway, but except for the occasional deer hidden in the trees, we saw only vast expanses of landscape – lakes and foothills, and later, great purple mountains, rising thousands of metres into the sky, jagged and glorious and strange.

Moosie was oddly silent. Once or twice we had to stop to pull his antlers out from under the headrest when they got stuck, but otherwise he slept. We hadn't really talked about the reason for the trip, trusting the time and the place to do the talking for us. Moosie needed a mate and a bigger back garden, and this was the best way we could think of to make him happy.

'How much longer?' We had been driving for nearly twelve hours on top of the long flight, and we all felt pretty strung out. I longed to stretch my legs and sleep lying down.

'Almost there,' Nick said, holding the map for me to see, his thumb and forefinger indicating how close we were to our destination.

* * * *

47

The cabin looked exactly as it had on the web page, made of logs, snug and solid, with a huge woodpile stacked in the lean-to at the side. Inside, it was decorated with Indian rugs, basic pine furniture and fat woollen blankets folded up on the beds. Everything was a little dusty and smelled of mouse; our cabin was a day's drive from just about any place you'd ever want to go, so I guessed it wasn't rented very often.

We piled wood into the big iron stove and started a fire, which heated the water and took the chill off the place. Moosie galloped in one door and out the other in a state of high excitement, barely able to contain his joy. He bucked and stomped and made little happy whinnying noises, and when we sent him out to explore, he didn't come back for hours.

'It's the right thing we're doing,' I murmured to Nick that night, tucked up in our birchwood bunks. 'And not just for us. For *him*. Look how happy he is here. He's not too big here, or too awkward.'

'Who'll make his breakfast and help him load his iPod?' Nick's voice was heavy with remorse. 'He loves Legoland. I never took him to see the Changing of the Guard.'

'He'll be back all the time to visit,' I said, knowing it wasn't true.

* * * *

I woke next morning to the smell of bacon and eggs and fresh-brewed coffee. Nick had been up since dawn, exploring the surrounding woods. He sounded just like a kid himself.

'The pines are gigantic,' he called, 'and I saw a beaver! There's a beautiful lake just below here, come see – and we've got a canoe. The note from the rental agent says it comes with the house. Look at the sky, Jess! We don't have that much blue in all of England.'

I was feeling a little blue myself, and it took a hell

of an effort to prise myself out of bed. Of course I wanted to see all the cool stuff Nick was talking about, but part of me couldn't quite face the day. We were liars and cheats, and poor Moosie thought we were just his loving parents, taking him on holiday. I climbed down from the top bunk, practising my cheerful smile. Nick seemed so happy that I wondered if I'd have to leave him behind, too.

All that day we canoed and lay in the sun while Moosie set off on longer and longer expeditions. At first he'd wander off for half an hour, bounding back to be near us, or to munch twigs in the shade of a tree. He waded into the lake and stood motionless for a long time, his nose just touching the water. But next time he set off it was hours before he returned, and then before we knew it, it was sundown, and we hadn't seen him since lunchtime.

'Do you think he's OK?' Nick looked gutted.

I nodded.

'What about predators?'

'What predators?'

'Mountain lions. Bears. Eagles.'

'Eagles?'

Nick frowned. 'Remember that programme where great hunkering eagles swooped down and pecked out your eyeballs?'

'It was vultures. Anyway, he'll be fine. He's a big boy now.' Too big for an eagle to fly off with, Nick, you muppet. But I understood his anxiety. Maybe this was it. Maybe we'd never see our boy again. I felt a strange mixture of sorrow and excitement. So much life lay ahead of him. And us.

By midnight he still wasn't back. Nick and I lay together, sleepless, straining for sounds in the vast woodland. Nature had never seemed so dark and terrifying as it did that night, luring creatures into its deepest heart and keeping them there with the promise of freedom. It was only the likes of us who didn't belong here. We felt guilty, like trespassers, and thought of Moosie, who had been a sort of trespasser to our way of life all along.

'Do you suppose he's found some sort of den to sleep in?'

'I don't think moose make dens.' You'd think the boy's own father might have checked his Wikipedia entry in three years.

Nick paused. 'Or someone to sleep *with*?'

Whether your son is an eighteen-year-old couch potato or a three-year-old moose doesn't much matter when it comes to the subject of sex. I couldn't bring myself to think of my velvety baby rutting away with some local townie tart of a moose girl. But that's what all this was about.

And who was I to talk, anyway?

* * * *

The trip back was subdued. As the big new 757 taxied for take-off, Nick and I held hands, shed a few tears and shivered a little in our crate in the hold. Life never turned out as you expected it to – we'd certainly learned *that* lesson.

Moosie and Missy were in first class; we'd had to max out on Nick's parents' credit card just for that. We could imagine them, snorting their passion over smoked salmon sandwiches and expensive toiletries.

We agreed that Moosie's girlfriend seemed nice – she had long legs, thick lashes and a wide, friendly mouth. I'd never seen Moosie look so happy and I hoped she wasn't just using him to get her EU passport.

But like I said, life never stops surprising you. A few weeks later, Missy announced that she was pregnant. Mum thought it was hilarious that I was going to be a grandma before my twenty-first birthday. But after the initial shock, I actually began to fancy the idea of a little pink grandbaby with a button nose and no underarm hair. Genetically speaking, the doctors agreed it was a perfectly likely outcome.

And boy, wouldn't I just *love* to see the look on their big moosey mugs eight months from now, if a homo sapien dropped out.

The last laugh was still up for grabs.

Extract from
Just in Case

Justin (formerly David) Case had work to do. He had to change how he looked, exchange David's baggy jeans and sweatshirts, his trainers and T-shirts, his unexceptional socks and mediocre anorak for the sort of clothes Justin Case might wear. In four months he would turn sixteen. He had always imagined everything would change when he turned sixteen, so why not start now?

He headed for the front door and found Charlie in the hall, balancing a small plastic hippo on the edge of a porcelain umbrella stand. Charlie looked up at his brother, startled, and dropped the animal into the abyss.

'Never mind.'

Justin reached into the deep cylinder and felt around for the toy, bringing it up with a handful of others. 'There's your hippo,' he said, placing it in his brother's outstretched hand. 'And a zebra, lion, goat, giraffe, cow. Why don't you play somewhere else? There's a whole lost animal kingdom down there.'

I'm not playing, Charlie said, dropping them back down the umbrella stand one by one. I'm thinking about falling.

Justin shook his head. Young children seemed unable to grasp the simplest principles. 'Suit yourself,' he said, ruffling the child's hair, and opening the door, set off down the road.

For the practicalities of his transformation he had chosen a nearby charity shop. Inside were thousands of cast-offs from other lives; surely one of them would fit him.

He walked the short distance to the shop feeling guilty and somewhat suspect, like a spy. The feeling was good. He had a mission.

Inside he hesitated, running his eyes over the racks of dowdy blouses, last decades' dresses, and partially scuffed shoes. The woman at the till, pinch-faced and scowling, glared at him but said nothing. In her eyes, he was obviously a shiftless, thieving young person with nothing better to do with the last days of his summer holiday than defraud charity shops of their chipped and valueless merchandise.

He stared back at her, eyes hard and emptied of emotion. The name was Case. Justin Case. If he wanted to try on a shirt, he would try on a shirt.

In the far corner, he spied a rack of men's clothing, crossed the floor to it and pulled out a shirt. He held it up under his chin. It smelled of something, something not entirely unpleasant, but not pleasant either. Stale cigarettes, burnt potatoes, coconut soap. The thought of adopting another person's smell hadn't occurred to him, made him faintly queasy. He closed his eyes, trying to expel the image from his brain.

A voice at his elbow nearly caused him to jump out of his skin. 'Try this,' the voice said, its arm holding out a dark brown and lavender paisley shirt.

Justin turned slowly. The voice belonged to a girl of perhaps nineteen, who peered at him through a heavy, clipped pink fringe. Her eyes were thickly rimmed with black kohl; her mouth neatly outlined in a vivid shade of orange that clashed perfectly with her hair. She wore four-inch platform boots in pale green snakeskin, wildly patterned tights, a very short skirt, and a tight see-through shirt printed with Japanese cartoons over which was squeezed a 1950s-style long-line beige elastic bra. A camera bag hung from her shoulder.

Even Justin recognized that her dress sense was unusual. 'Wow,' he said.

'Thank you,' she replied demurely. And then, 'I've never seen you before.' She tilted her head to one side, taking in his pale skin, lank hair and good cheekbones. The dark circles under his eyes.

Doomed youth, she thought. Interesting.

Justin looked alarmed. 'What?'

'I was just thinking. You could find some excellent things here if you knew what to look for.'

'I know what I need.'

She waited.

'Everything,' he said at last. 'Everything different in every way from this.' He indicated himself.

'Everything?'

'Yes. I need a whole new identity.'

'Have you killed someone?' She smiled.

He met her eyes. 'Not yet.'

The perfectly drawn orange mouth formed a tiny 'o'.

Justin turned away. When he looked back, she was still staring at him.

'You're a *potential* killer?'

He sighed. 'A potential kill-ee, more like.'

Her eyes narrowed. 'Are you involved with drugs?'

'No.'

'Blackmail?'

'No.'

'Witness protection?'

'No.'

'Spooks?'

He shook his head. 'No, nothing like that.'

'Then what?'

Justin fidgeted, shifting his weight from one foot to another. He tapped his foot. Chewed his thumb. 'I discovered my old self was doomed.'

'Doomed?'

'Doomed.'

'In what sense, doomed?'

'In the sense of standing poised on the brink of ruin with time running out.'

She stared.

'Which is why I need to change everything, all of me. I can't be recognized.'

The girl frowned. 'But who do you think will recognize you?'

He dropped his voice. 'Fate. My fate. David Case's fate, that is.'

'Who's David Case?'

'Me. That is, I used to be him. Before I started changing everything.'

'You've changed your name?'

He nodded.

'So, you're running away from fate,' the girl said slowly, 'and you think all this is going to make a difference?'

He shrugged. 'What else can I do?'

'Stop believing in fate?'

Justin sighed. 'I wish I could.'

Neither of them said anything for a long time. The girl studied a chip on one of her nails.

'Well,' she said finally, with the smallest hint of a smile. 'It's *different*.'

He smiled back.

'Not uninteresting,' she added.

'Not?'

'No.' She raised an eyebrow. '*Not*.'

She extended her hand. 'My name is Agnes.' The fingers she offered had pale green fingernails.

'Justin. Justin Case.'

She blinked, digesting this information. And then all at once she beamed, her face illuminated with delight. He took the hand she offered. It was surprisingly soft and warm, and he held it cautiously, not sure when to let go. He had no experience of touching older women.

'How very nice to meet you, Justin Case.'

Still smiling, Agnes turned to one of the racks and pulled out a shirt: poppy-coloured, long sleeves, ruffle down the front. She thrust it at Justin, along with the brown and lavender paisley.

'Try these. I'll keep looking.'

Justin looked at the shirts. 'I don't think so.'

She ignored him.

Justin sighed, took the hangers, and entered the tiny changing room at the far end of the shop. There was barely room to turn sideways.

The first shirt fitted. He buttoned it and looked around for a mirror.

Agnes swept the curtain aside and Justin found himself viewed in reverse close-up portrait through the wrong end of a Nikon 55mm DX lens. Click click click, click click click. Three frames per second. Two seconds. He leapt back with a startled squeak.

Agnes's face emerged from one side of her Nikon. 'What?'

'What do you mean "what?" *That.*'

She frowned. 'Turn round and let me look at you.'

He turned round and let her look at him.

'Not bad.' She beamed approval, then put down the camera and picked up a small pile of clothes. 'I've been keeping an eye on these things for ages. For exactly the right person.'

The thought of being exactly the right person appealed to Justin so completely that he tried everything she brought him and attempted to like it all. She brought him a turquoise flowered shirt, a skinny brown cardigan that he thought must have been designed for a woman, and a pair of white canvas trousers that had to be cinched with a belt. He put them all on and emerged from the cubicle, nervous.

Click click, click click click. Five shots aimed with deadly accuracy at his head. Agnes lowered her camera and considered him. 'Excellent. You'll take them all.' She squinted, her head turned slightly to one side. 'You're very lucky I was here today.'

Justin nodded uncertainly.

'Of course, this is only the beginning.' She spotted a red and white vinyl bowling bag and crossed briskly to pick it up. Justin watched her. He had no idea what she was talking about, but the feeling fitted with his new life as a stranger. There was even something reassuring about it.

Agnes carried the clothes to the till, accepted a small pile of creased £5 notes from Justin and handed them to the sour-faced woman. The money looked as if it had been crammed in a piggy bank for years, which it had. 'That's all he has,' she told the scowling troll. 'It'll have to do.'

While the woman harrumphed and muttered irritably, Agnes flicked through her camera's digital display.

She looked up and gazed solemnly at Justin. 'You photograph like an angel, Justin Case.'

Was he being solicited for a child pornography website, or perhaps a fanzine article on fashion disasters?

'Never mind. Next time I'll bring proofs.'

Next time?

'I've enjoyed our first meeting immensely.'

He tried to smile, but it came out lopsided, uncertain. Click click click.

On the way out of the shop, Agnes spied a pair of pristine black jeans half-hidden under a pile of shirts. She stopped short, examined them and tossed them to Justin.

'Try them on.'

She waited outside the tiny changing room as he pulled them on. They fitted perfectly.

Agnes swept back the curtain once more. 'Could you scream?' she asked happily.

Justin nodded. He thought he probably could.

Extract from
What I Was

It all began on the coast of East Anglia, past the indentation where the River Ore ran salt and melted into the sea. There, a bit of land stuck out from the mainland, a small peninsula roughly shaped like a rat's nose. In maps (old maps) this peninsula was labelled The Stele, after a seventh-century commemorative stone marker, or stele, found very near to school property in 1825.

The letter my school sent to prospective parents contained a three-quarter page description of the area. Location was a selling point (salt air contributes to strong lungs and clear minds) and elegant italics explained how the stele was found half-buried in earth, the stone large and heavy and probably transported from Lindisfarne on the Northumbrian coast. Such markers were not uncommon in this part of the country, but this one boasted an excellent carved portrait of St Oswald, a seventh-century king of Britain, with the Anglo-Saxon equivalent of Oswald was here carved on it. The stone itself is long gone, moved to the British Museum.

St Oswald's School for Boys, which you won't have heard of, was situated two miles inland. The school road ran between the A-road and the coast in a more or less straight line, with a footpath running parallel for most of its length. At the sea, the road turned left (north), while the footpath turned right (south). Following the footpath, you could reach The Stele in about twenty minutes – or at least you could reach the canal of deep water that separated it from the mainland. For only a few hours a day, when the tide was very low, the little peninsula could be accessed via a damp sand causeway. All around it, salt marsh and reed beds provided homes for nesting waders and waterfowl – oyster catchers, little terns, cormorants, gulls – and had once done the same for Iceni, Roman, Saxon and Viking settlers.

A few miles and a million light years away was my home from home, Mogg House, a four-storey building with studies (tiny as tombs) on the bottom floor, communal dormitories in the middle, and bedrooms with living rooms on the floors above. Boys my age lived on the top floor in rooms designed for two, which now housed four, thanks to our bursar's desire to maximize revenues. Loos were located on the ground floor, and to this day I believe I retain exceptional bladder control thanks to the inconvenience of the conveniences. It was something we developed with time and practice, like proficiency in maths or arpeggio technique.

Despite the brutality of the coastal winters, we lived without heat. Warmth was considered antithetical to the development of the immune system and we were expected to possess an almost superhuman tolerance for cold. On a positive note, the conditions at my previous school – situated two hundred miles further north – had been worse. There, we kept warm in winter by sleeping in our clothes, in woollen jerseys, socks and trousers with pyjamas layered on top, and awoke most mornings to banks of snow under the open windows and ice in the toilets.

At St Oswald's, we fell out of bed at the sound of a bell, buttoned a clean collar (if we had one) on to our shirts, pulled on yesterday's underwear, flannel trousers, socks and heavy black shoes, and headed downstairs for a breakfast of grey porridge and cold toast. Post-war rationing had finished eight years before, but the habit of mean, depressing food lingered in school kitchens throughout the land. After breakfast came chapel, then five lessons on the trot without a break, followed by lunch (pink sausages, green liver, brown stew, cabbage boiled to stinking transparency), followed by an afternoon dedicated to sport or the tedium of cadet parade, followed by supper, followed by prep, followed by bed.

Beneath this relatively straightforward schedule lurked the shady regions of school life where the real dramas were played out, where elaborate hierarchies established life's winners and losers, ranking each carefully according to the ill-defined caste system of school life. As in the outside world, social mobility barely existed; one's status at the start determined whether life would be filled with misery or triumph. I don't recall any boy improving his lot significantly in the course of his school years, though perhaps memory fails me.

'Oi, you!'

Three days in. I emerged from my own thoughts to meet the gaze of an imperious Upper Sixth.

'*You!*'

Yes, I sighed inwardly. *Me*.

'What's that?' He pointed to the bottom button of my school blazer.

It's a woodpecker, you creeping maggot.

He reached over with calm deliberation and tore the button off. It's worth noting that this required considerable effort. And left a large hole. In my new. Blazer.

'*Un*buttoned,' he spat. 'Understood?'

I stared.

'The correct answer, scum, is *Yes, sir*.'

'Yes, sir.' I had learnt to imbue a lack of sarcasm with infinite subtlety.

He turned on his heel and stalked off, while I scrabbled in the grass for my button. I felt no particular shame, having encountered dozens of chippy little fascists in my time, but continued to wonder at their delusions.

Our world revolved around school rules, rules as mysterious and arcane as the murkier corners of a papal cabal. Bottom button of blazer open or not,

left hand in pocket or not, diagonal or straight crossing of the courtyard, running or walking on the lawn,
books in right hand or left, blue ink or black, cap
tipped forward or back. There was no crib sheet,
no list to consult, no house book embossed *Rules*.
Regulations merely existed, bobbing to the surface
of school life like turds. We took their randomness,
their rigidity, their sheer number, for granted and we
obeyed because they were there, because we were
newer or younger or weaker than the enforcers, because to fill our heads with more meaningful information might require the use of our critical
faculties. Which would lead to doubts about the
whole system. Which would lead to social and
economic collapse and the end of life as we knew it.

It was easier just to get on with it.

Let me be clear: many boys (popular, clever, athletic)
had a perfectly happy time at St Oswald's; I simply
was not one of them. And yet I had certain attributes
– a face that hid emotion, a healthy contempt for fair

play – that served me well. I was not destined for glittering prizes, but I was not without qualities.

Our lessons took place beneath the draughty high ceilings of the main school building, always accompanied by the random clatter and crash of nineteenth-century plumbing. Day after day, I sat with an earnest but uncomprehending look on my face, knowing that it was exactly this expression that made teachers skip to the boy on my left. They hated explaining things over and over – it bored them, caused them to despise their lives.

Despite (or perhaps because of) the depressing familiarity of these conditions, I settled into St Oswald's at once.

One of the more notable facts about the stretch of coastline I have just described is that it is sinking at great speed.

This is the sort of fact about which it has become fashionable to panic in the middle of the twenty-first century, when nearly everyone agrees that our planet is on its last legs, but it has been true of this stretch of land for at least a thousand years. In contrast, the opposite coast in Wales is rising, which suggests that all of England is slowly tipping into the sea. Once the eastern coast sinks low enough and the western rises high enough, the entire country will slip gently under water in a flurry of bubbles and formal protests from the House of Lords. I greatly look forward to this gentle slipping into oblivion and believe it will do our nation no end of good.

Back then I might not have agreed. For one thing, I was less interested in geological catastrophe. For another, my contemporaries and I tended to view the future as a vast blank slate on which to write our own version of human history. But all this took a back seat to the real work that occupied each day – perfecting our lines for the drama of school life. It was important to be able to perform them without thinking – the not talking back, the respectful dipping of the head to teachers, the unsarcastic 'sir', the stepping aside for bigger boys.

I rarely thought about the schools I'd left behind; whatever impression they had made had been all bad – hard work, too much sport, disgusting food and a proud tradition of sadism. Getting ejected from the first had been effortless, requiring nothing more than an enthusiastic disdain for deadlines and games. Even without much of a reputation to uphold, they were pleased to see me go.

Expulsion from the second required slightly more effort and the help of materials readily available from any school chemistry lab.

It occurred to me, however, that falling out of favour with St Oswald's (which specialized in low expectations) might be more difficult. Even the teaching staff, a ragtag bunch of cripples and psychological refugees, appeared to have few prospects elsewhere. Mr Barnes, a victim of shell shock with a prosthetic bottom and one eye, taught history. He had occasional good days during which he spoke with almost thrilling animation about battles and treaties and doomed royal successions, but the rest of the time he merely sat at the front of the class and stared at his hands. From motives having nothing to do with compassion we left him alone on his black days, tiptoeing out so that his classroom echoed with silence by the time the bell rang.

Thomas Thomas, a refugee from All Souls, Oxford, with a stutter and lofty ideals, attempted fruitlessly to seduce our souls with the poetry of Wordsworth and Keats. Even without the idiotic name he'd have been branded a victim; with it, of course, he was doomed. We all knew his type: tall, dreamy and peevish, author of an unfinished novel destined to remain unfinished forever. It was easy to make him weep with frustration until he got the hang of school life, at which point (despite his aesthete tendencies and long white hands), he became our year's most enthusiastic applier of the cane.

M. Markel was always willing to set translations aside to recount his experiences with the maquisards, his comrades in the French resistance. We adored tales of torture and self-sacrifice under Vichy rule, but never heard one through to the end. The stories inflamed his passions to such a degree that, partway in, he would lapse into the impenetrable Basque patois of his youth.

The rest barely deserve mention. Mr Brandt (dull). Mr Lindsay (effeminate). Mr Harper (hairpiece, vain). Last, and least, was the dreaded Mr Beeson, headmaster (thick), who also taught RE. It's not that we thought we deserved a Mr Chips-type head (kindly, bespectacled, inspiring), but Mr Beeson barely topped five foot two, had the ruddy, un-imaginative face of a butcher's apprentice, and cherished a private passion for Napoleonic battle re-enactments that far exceeded any interest he had in the teaching profession. Rumour had it that he had gained the post due to the unfortunate shortage of candidates in the years following the war. The fact that his knowledge of Latin and Greek seemed scarcely better than our own bore this out.

Have I forgotten to mention sport? Daily drilling in cricket or rugby took place under the relentless eye of Mr Parkhouse, who was a fiend for what he called 'conditioning'. This entailed long runs across the muddy countryside on days when weather conditions prevented actual games. I can still hear the dull thud of all those feet, more than eighty at a time, propelled by sweaty thighs and wildly swinging arms, clambering through hedges and over stiles, too tired to express resentment but not too tired to feel it. To vary the routine we sometimes ran along the beach, panting along the damp sand in twos and threes until cramp or insurrection put an end to forward motion.

It is always Reese I think of when remembering these runs. He had taken to seeking me out, trailing me like a shadow, mistaking the person least interested in tormenting him for a friend. He had a disturbing tendency to pop up in exactly the place I least expected him to be, tangling my feet like a jungle snare, and most of the time all I wanted was to shake him off.

This combination of unwanted exercise and unwelcome company occasionally caused me to call a halt to the entire proceedings – once I lay flat behind a stand of trees, another time I crouched among the reeds until the thundering mass of boys disappeared from view. At those times, I felt a profound sense of release as I wandered back, admiring the mackerel sky and the soft silent swoop of owls.

This particular September morning was warm and intermittently sunny. Gold and purple heather set the marshes ablaze, and beyond lay the dark green surface of the sea. The low tide had created a long stretch of clear sand between the beach and The Stele, and Mr Parkhouse led us out on to the causeway at a brisk gallop. My breath, hoarse and loud, drowned the outraged calls of shore birds. Ahead was a small group of abandoned fishermen's shacks, mostly locked up and rotting with blacked-out windows. As we rounded the point, a feeling that irreparable damage had been done to my Achilles tendon made it clear that I should sit down, and I took advantage of the first shack to disappear from view.

As the rest of the boys ran on, Reese jogged on the spot, his desperate smile twisted into an unintentional leer. 'What you doing?'

'Bugger off,' I answered. He turned beet red and legged it.

A dreamy silence settled on the spot. I lay slumped against the shack watching the soft rise and fall of waves, silencing my own breathing until there was no sound and nothing left in the world except sand and sea and sky. After a few minutes, the cloud cover gave way to a burst of brilliant sunlight and the slow dull sea leapt with diamonds.

The voice when it came was clear, oddly inflected, not unfriendly.

'What are you doing here?'

I looked up, startled. In front of me stood a person about my own age, with black eyes and a quizzical expression. He was slim, slightly taller than average and barefoot, his thick dark hair unfashionably shaggy. A heavy, old-fashioned fisherman's sweater topped baggy long shorts, chopped down from trousers and rolled.

He looked impossibly familiar, like a fantasy version of myself, with the face I had always hoped would look back at me from a mirror. The bright, flickering quality of his skin reminded me of the surface of the sea. He was almost unbearably beautiful and I had to turn away, overcome with pleasure and longing and a realization of life's desperate unfairness.

'I'm sorry,' I managed to stutter, pulling myself to my feet.

He gazed at me, taking in the exposed, blue-white schoolboy flesh, the stiff cotton shorts, the aertex vest plastered with sweat. From behind him a small grey cat gazed, its tail erect and twitching, as if testing the atmosphere for spies. Both looked, and neither shouted at me to leave. I took this as encouragement.

'I don't suppose I might bother you for –' I fought for an excuse, any reason to stay – 'some water?'

The boy hesitated, reluctant rather than unsure, then shrugged, turned, and disappeared into the little shack. The cat stalked behind him, crossing one delicate paw in front of the other as he went. I followed, delighted and amazed by this unexpected turn of events. Compared to the beautiful boy and the cat I felt scruffy and crass, but I didn't mind, being not unused to scraping dignity out of pathos.

It took a moment for my eyes to adjust to the interior of the hut. There were only two rooms: a tiny sitting room at the front facing the sea and an equally small kitchen overlooking the reed beds. Flattened, nearly colourless rugs covered rough pine boards, and the chipped remnants of a once-fine set of china sat neatly on wooden shelves in the kitchen. Two smallish front windows opened on to sweeping views of the sea. Across the room, a narrow staircase led to what I assumed was a sleeping loft; a shallow pitched roof indicated that the space would be cramped. Beneath the stairs, a cupboard closed with a worn wooden latch. Simply framed photographs hung in uneven intervals on the wall above the staircase: a bearded man with a weathered face. A portrait of a young woman. A fishing boat. A shire horse.

All black and white. All, decades old.

The low, banked fire in the iron stove threw off enough heat to make the hut feel warm and comforting as soup. Settled in front of the stove, the cat never took its eyes off me.

'You can sit if you like,' said the boy in a slightly

stilted voice, as if he didn't speak English fluently or perhaps had lost the habit of speaking. He poured water from a large metal tin into a kettle and placed it on one of the burners.

I thought of the dreary Victorian schoolrooms of St Oswald's, of the freezing brick dormitories, of my parents' home with its gloomy semi-rural respectability. This place was unassuming and intimate, its spirit soft, worn and warmed by decades of use. It was as if I had fallen through a small tear in the universe, down the rabbit hole, into some idealized version of This Boy's Life.

Remembering what I had in the way of manners, I gave the boy my name and he didn't flinch – a rare enough reaction, and one I appreciated. Panic began to overtake me at the thought of having to drink my cup of tea and return to the reality of school food and school rules and school life. I sat, photographing the scene with my eyes and looking around for signs that the boy lived here with a grown-up of some description. The hut was very small, but also very tidy. The floors were free of sand, and there were none of the usual cheery beach relics crowded on to window sills. The cotton rugs, though worn, were immaculate. A large pyramid of wood had been stacked neatly beside the stove.

Not a detail out of place.

The boy returned to the little sitting room carrying a teacup with roses on it. 'It's black,' he said, handing me the tea, with no apparent desire to know if that would do.

'Thank you.' I raised the cup and gulped a mouthful of hot tea. 'Do you live here alone?'

He did not welcome questions, this much was clear. Without answering, he turned back to the kitchen, followed by the cat. I waited for him to volunteer an explanation, but it didn't come so I jabbered instead, uncomfortable with silence.

'I'm at St Oswald's, a boarder. It's diabolical,' I said, in an effort to prove somehow that I was *on his side*. 'I hate studying and I'm no good at sport. It's cold all the time and the food is inedible. It's the most idiotic waste of time.' I looked up from my tea, anxious for sympathy. 'And money.'

He appeared not to be listening.

'Do you have a name?' I asked.

'Finn,' said the boy.

'Nice to meet you, Finn.'

I finished my tea slowly, but once it was gone could think of no reason to stay. 'I'd better go then,' I said, with what sounded even to me like a lack of conviction.

'Goodbye,' Finn said and I felt like weeping.

Outside, I turned to wave, but Finn had already shut the door on our encounter. Back at school I'd missed breakfast, chapel, and the beginning of Latin. Which meant detention and fifty extra lines.

And bothered me not at all.

Bright and shiny and sizzling with fun stuff ...

puffin.co.uk

WEB FUN

UNIQUE and exclusive digital content!
Podcasts, photos, Q&A, Day in the Life of, interviews
and much more, from Eoin Colfer, Cathy Cassidy,
Allan Ahlberg and Meg Rosoff to Lynley Dodd!

WEB NEWS

The **Puffin Blog** is packed with posts and photos from
Puffin HQ and special guest bloggers. You can also sign up
to our monthly newsletter **Puffin Beak Speak**

WEB CHAT

Discover something new EVERY month –
books, competitions and treats galore

WEBBED FEET

(Puffins have funny little feet and
brightly coloured beaks)

Point your mouse our way today!

It all started with a Scarecrow.

Puffin is seventy years old.
Sounds ancient, doesn't it? But Puffin has never been
so lively. We're always on the lookout for the next big
idea, which is how it began all those years ago.

Penguin Books was a big idea from the mind of
a man called Allen Lane, who in 1935 invented
the quality paperback and changed the world.
**And from great Penguins, great Puffins grew,
changing the face of children's books forever.**

The first four Puffin Picture Books were hatched in 1940 and the
first Puffin story book featured a man with broomstick arms called
Worzel Gummidge. In 1967 Kaye Webb, Puffin Editor, started the
Puffin Club, promising to **'make children into readers'**.
She kept that promise and over 200,000 children became
devoted Puffineers through their quarterly instalments of
Puffin Post, which is now back for a new generation.

Many years from now, we hope you'll look back and
remember Puffin with a smile. **No matter what your age
or what you're into, there's a Puffin for everyone.**
The possibilities are endless, but one thing is for sure:
whether it's a picture book or a paperback, a sticker book
or a hardback, **if it's got that little Puffin
on it – it's bound to be good.**